T0273114

PSILOCYBIN PRODUCTION

Psilocybe cubensis cultivated indoors

PSILOCYBIN PRODUCTION

*Producing Organic Psilocybin
in a Small Room*

Adam Gottlieb

RONIN PUBLISHING, INC.

www.roninpub.com

PSILOCYBIN PRODUCTION

ISBN: 0-914171-92-5

ISBN: 978-0-914171-92-8

Copyright © 1997 by Twentieth Century Alchemist & Ronin Publishing, Inc.

Project Editor: Sebastian Orfali

Editors: Adam Gottlieb, Bob Harris, and Sebastian Orfali

Cover Design: Judy July

Front Cover Photo: Bob Harris

Back Cover Photo: Adam Gottlieb

Published by:

RONIN PUBLISHING, INC.

P.O. Box 3436

Oakland, CA 94609

www.roninpub.com

First printing 1997

Printed in the United States of America

Distributed by PGW-Ingram

Library of Congress Card Number: 2002095314

Notice to Reader

Picture Credits

front cover: photo by Bob Harris

p. i, iii: illustration by Larry Todd

p. ii: photo by Adam Gottlieb

p. viii: photo by Allan Richardson

p. 2: illustration from *Design Motifs of Ancient Mexico* (Enciso, 1953)

p. 6: photo by Adam Gottlieb

p. 9: illustration by Michael B. Smith from *Hallucinogenic and Poisonous Mushroom Field Guide* (Menser, 1997)

p. 15: illustrations by Michael B. Smith from *Hallucinogenic and Poisonous Mushroom Field Guide* (Menser, 1997)

p. 19: illustrations by Michael B. Smith from *Hallucinogenic and Poisonous Mushroom Field Guide* (Menser, 1997)

p. 21: illustration from The Complete Encyclopedia of Illustration (Heck, 1979)

p. 22: illustrations by Michael B. Smith from *Hallucinogenic and Poisonous Mushroom Field Guide* (Menser, 1997)

p. 24: illustration from The Complete Encyclopedia of Illustration (Heck, 1979)

p. 26: illustration by Larry Todd; effects by David Wells

p. 28: illustration from *Alchemy* (Fabricius, 1976)

p. 30: illustration by Larry Todd

p. 34: illustration from The Complete Encyclopedia of Illustration (Heck, 1979)

p. 38: photo by Adam Gottlieb

p. 42: illustration from *Alchemy* (Fabricius, 1976)

p. 47: illustration by Larry Todd

p. 48: illustration from *Alice's Adventures Under Ground* (Carroll, 1985)

p. 52: illustration by Larry Todd

p. 55: illustration by Larry Todd

p. 57: photo by Adam Gottlieb

p. 60: photo by Bob Harris

p. 68: illustration from *Design Motifs of Ancient Mexico* (Enciso, 1953)

back cover: photo by Adam Gottlieb

Quoted Text Credits

p. viii: as quoted in *Plants of the Gods* (Schultes & Hofmann, 1992)

p. 27: from *The Practical Handbook of Plant Alchemy* (Junius, 19?)

p. 44: from *Pharmacotheon* (Ott, 1993)

p. 48: from *Alice's Adventures Under Ground* (Carroll, 1985)

p. 58: from *The Doors of Perception* (Huxley, 1954)

p. 67: from *Teonanácatl* (Ott & Bigwood, 1978)

Table of Contents

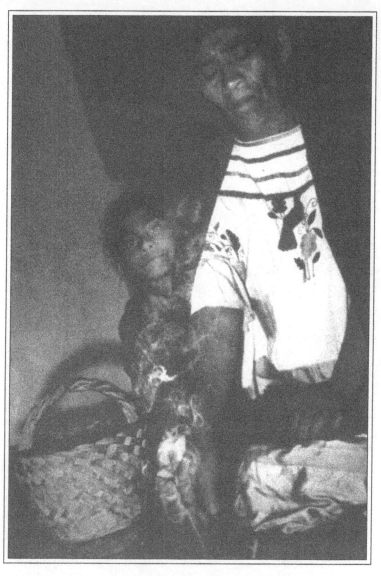

Allan Richardson

"*The sacred mushroom takes me by the hand and brings me to the world where everything is known. It is they, the sacred mushrooms, that speak in a way I can understand.*"

—**Mexican shaman María Sabina**

Introduction

It is not difficult to cultivate the mycelium of any of the psychoactive bearing mushrooms for a person who knows how to do it. The mycelium is the fibrous underground network of the mushroom. The familiar stem and cap portions of the mushrooms are called carpophores. The mycelium can be readily grown in ordinary Mason™ jars in a low cost medium in 10 to 12 days and the active materials (psilocybin and psilocin) can be extracted.

This book explains how all of these steps are carried out on a small or large scale. Complete descriptions are given for locating the mushrooms; developing stock cultures for inoculation; cultivating, harvesting, and drying the mycelium; extracting the active alkaloids; and using existing cultures to seed new cultures in order to maintain an ongoing psilocybin farm which can yield a regular crop of the hallucinogenic mycelium. Descriptions are also given of a process for setting up in a small workroom a large scale psilocybin factory. Finally, there is a brief overview of the procedures involved in the fruiting of the mushroom mycelium.

Psilocybin and the Law

 It is difficult to determine how the use of certain hallucinogenic substances would be treated in the courts. Possession of psilocybin and psilocin (misspelled in the U.S. code as "psilocyn") is a felony under Title 21, Section I, (C) of the United States Code (1970 Edition). *Psilocybe mexicana* is also illegal. There was sufficient ignorance on the part of the law makers not to include the many other mushroom species containing psilocybin and psilocin.

Theoretically, the possession of any psilocybin-bearing mushroom would be the same as possessing the alkaloid itself. But when it comes to prosecution it does not necessarily work like that. Lysergic acid amides—which occur in morning glory seeds, stems, and leaves—are also illegal, but there is no way to prevent gardeners from raising this ornamental flower.

It is illegal for anyone in the USA to possess mescaline. Peyote, which contains mescaline, is legal for bonafide members of the Native American Church when used ritualistically, but no member may possess extracts of the cactus or the drug mescaline. Peyote is illegal for nonmembers, but San Pedro and several other species of *Trichocereus* cacti also contain mescaline and are available from many legitimate cactus dealers.

It would be considered illegal for anyone to extract the active principles from any of the above mentioned plants. And it would be considered illegal for anyone to extract psilocybin and psilocin from mushrooms or mycelium as described in this book. Anyone found operating a large scale mycelium farm could be prosecuted for intent to manufacture psilocybin and psilocin. There are also many different state laws which must be considered before doing anything with psilocybin-bearing mushrooms. There are, however, many nations which have no laws regarding these substances.

The foregoing is not a thorough interpretation of the law. Rather these points are mentioned to give some indication of the legal pitfalls which surround the application of the

The present drug laws are a pathetic mess. The old adage that ignorance of the law is no excuse becomes a ludicrous statement when the laws themselves are rooted in ignorance. One classical example of this is the classification of the stimulant cocaine as a narcotic. One is reminded of the king in Alice in Wonderland who made up his own language as he went along with total disregard for the accepted definitions of words. I will not even go into the question of whether any law enforcement agency has the moral or Constitutional right to dictate what substances we may or may not take into our own adult bodies. Any modern individual whose mind is not immersed in the slavish dung pit of Dark Age unreasoning knows that reliable education—not criminal penalization—is the answer to whatever drug problems exist. Nevertheless, we must contend realistically with the powers that unfortunately be at this time. They are the ones with the badges, guns, gavels, and goons.

—Stone Kingdom Manifesto, 1976

activities described in this book. Furthermore, laws are constantly being revised. By the time this book is published and read the laws may have changed for better or for worse. The author and publisher are not recommending or endorsing the application of the information in this book, especially in places where there are laws proscribing these substances. This information is offered for the sake of pure knowledge, because it is a constitutional right to do so. The violation of any existing laws is not encouraged.

Psilocybe cubensis **cultivated indoors**

Finding Psilocybin Mushrooms

All it takes is one mushroom or a few spores. From this, one can quickly develop a culture that will continue to produce as much psilocybin as desired for years to come. Because the common San Ysidro mushroom *Psilocybe cubensis* (Singer), formerly *Stropharia cubensis* (Earl), is the most easily obtainable, most readily cultivated, most disease resistant, and psychoactively strongest species, the techniques in this book are geared to its use. There are, however, numerous other species which contain psilocybin. In case one of these other species is all that is available, pertinent information for several of them is given: such as relative potency; where and when to find specimens; what growing conditions (medium, temperature, lighting, etc.) they favor; and how resistant they are to contamination.

The states, provinces, and regions named are by no means the only places where the species is to be found. They are places in which there have been numerous reports of findings. They are given here to give a general idea of the type of terrain and climate the species favors. In cases where ideal cultivation temperatures and growing conditions are not listed, much can be surmised by considering the environment in which that species thrives.

Psilocybe cubensis can be found in many parts of the United States, Mexico, Colombia, Australia, and even Southeast Asia. It is usually found growing on or near cow dung in pastures during warm rainy periods from February to November. There are several species of mushroom which occur on cow dung, but none of these bears much resemblance to the San Ysidro.

There are numerous toxic mushrooms growing in the wild. Some of these could be mistaken for some of the psilocybian fungi mentioned in this book. It is essential that the mushroom hunter learn to use an identification key. A key is a listing of various features which will positively identify a given species. CAUTION: If a specimen does not conform in every respect to the key, it must not be used. There are several excellent keys to be found on

Psilocybe cubensis
· ·.·-; by Michael B. Smith from *Hallucinogenic and Poisonous Mushroom Field Guide*
by Gary P. Menser, Ronin Publishing, Inc. Used by permission.

most library shelves. One that is highly recommend by mycologists is *Keys to Genera of Higher Fungi* by R. Shaffer, 2nd ed. (1968) published by the University of Michigan Biological Station at Ann Arbor. Also recommended is *Hallucinogenic and Poisonous Mushroom Field Guide* by Gary P. Menser, available from Ronin Publishing. It is further suggested that after the specimen is identified it should be brought to an expert mycologist in order to confirm its identity.

Testing the Mushroom

Many books on hallucinogenic mushrooms suggest a simple test for psilocybian species that involves breaking the flesh of the specimen and waiting about 30 minutes for a bluing reaction to take place. This bluing is due to the oxidation of indole based substances in the fungus. Although it is true that most of the psilocybin-bearing mushrooms will respond positively to this test, other species may also do the same. CAUTION : The poisonous *Eastwood Boletus* blues upon exposure of its inner tissues to oxygen just like any psilocybian mushroom. Another test that is often given in mushroom manuals is treating the exposed tissues with Metol, a chemical used in photo developers. It hastens the bluing of psilocybian mushrooms, and supposedly one can do a bluing test with it in a few minutes rather than the usual 30 minutes or more. Any mushroom, however, that contains indolic substances of any sort will respond positively to this test. Since indole-based amino acids such as tryptophan are found in most living organisms, this test is rather useless.

Actually, there is no field test for psilocybian mushrooms. There is, however, a relatively simple test for the presence of psilocin and psilocybin that can be carried out at home by anyone who has some familiarity with paper chromatography. The mushroom sample is dried, pulverized, and then extracted into a small amount of unheated methanol by shaking it for half an hour. After the debris in the methanol has settled, the paper is spotted with the top fluid in a zone about 2 mm wide. The spotting zone is then treated with water-saturated butanol for about 2 hours. If psilocin and psilocybin are present in the specimen, the resulting solvent front (7-8 cm from the initial spotting zone) will contain them. After drying

the paper with a half dryer set on warm, this
outer zone is sprayed lightly with a saturated
solution of p-dimethyl-aminobenzaldehyde in
alcohol and again with 1 N hydrochloric acid.
The paper is then dried as before. Where psilocybin is present, a reddish color will develop.
The presence of psilocin will be indicated by a
blue-violet zone.

Data on Various Psilocybian Species

Conocybe cyanopus: Found from May through September—usually in dense shade scattered among mosses and in wet soil around bogs, swamps, and ditches—in the northwestern USA and as far east as Michigan. Carpophores grow well in sphagnum moss having a pH range of 7-8.

Copelandia cyanescens: Found from early summer through late autumn—scattered, grouped, or clustered on cow dung or rich soil—in Florida and other southern states. Spores germinate easily on all agar media. Optimum growth occurs on MEA at 80° F. Carpophores can be produced on uncased compost or on rye.

Panaeolus foenisecii (also known as *Panaeolina foenisecii* or *Psilocybe foenisecii,* and commonly known as haymower's mushroom or harvest mushroom): Found in late spring and early summer or in July, August, and September during cool, wet seasons—scattered or grouped in large numbers on lawns, pastures, and other grassy places—throughout the USA and in Quebec. Tests of specimens found in Washington revealed no psilocybin, but eastern specimens were potent.

Panaeolus sphinctrinus: Found in summer and autumn—in small groups in forests, fields, and roadsides (almost always on cow dung)—in many temperate parts of the world.

Panaeolus subbalteatus: Found from spring through autumn—grouped or clustered (often in rings up to two feet in diameter) on open ground, freshly manured lawns, straw piles, all types of compost, dung piles, and roadsides—in Ontario and throughout the USA (especially in Massachusetts, Maryland, New York, Ohio, Michigan, Washington, and Oregon). Optimum growth in MEA is at 86° F. It occasionally occurs as a weed mushroom in commercial mushroom houses.

Pholiotina cyanopoda: Found from August through September—solitary or clustered on lawns—in such diverse parts of the USA as New York, Washington, and Colorado.

Psilocybe baeocystis: Found in autumn and winter—solitary, grouped, or clustered on earth,

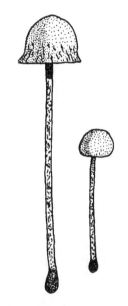

Conocybe cyanopus   *Panaeolus sphinctrinus*

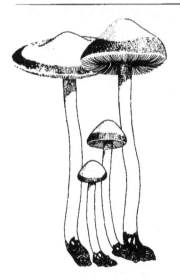

Panaeolus subbalteatus   *Psilocybe baeocystis*

Drawing by Michael B. Smith from *Hallucinogenic and Poisonous Mushroom Field Guide* by Gary P. Menser, Ronin Publishing, Inc. Used by permission.

lawns, mulch, and decomposing forest wood near scattered trees (especially conifers)—in western Oregon and Washington. It does well on all agar media at 77° F. This is a potent species containing psilocybin, psilocin, baeocystin, and nor-baeocystin. Perhaps it is because of the latter two alkaloids that it is the most visually hallucinogenic of the psilocybian mushrooms. There is a report that in 1960 a six-year old boy died after eating a large number of these mushrooms. There has never been any other indication that these alkaloids are dangerous. **CAUTION: People consuming *Psilocybe baeocystis* or any other species must proceed with caution.** Knowledgeable mycophiles start with small doses and progress gradually to larger ones. This is especially important when using the extracted crude alkaloids, which may contain large concentrations of the baeocystin alkaloids.

Psilocybe caerulescens: Found in summer during the rainy season—grouped or clustered (but rarely solitary) in shady places on soil, sugar cane mulch, recently turned earth, or stream banks—in Alabama, northern Florida, and Mexico. The Mexican variety *P. caerulescens var. mazatecorum* is known locally as *derrumbe,* which means "landslides." There it is often found among landslides or near corn and coffee plantations. The mycelium does best on MEA at 81° F. Thermal death occurs at 95° F. It is almost impossible to produce car- pophores on sterilized rye medium. They can be grown on vegetable compost in dim light, but the incubation period is long (55-85 days). Although this species is resistant to white mold, its long incubation period leaves it prone to other diseases. It is not one of the more potent species.

Psilocybe caerulipes: Found in summer and occasionally autumn—solitary or clustered on decomposing logs and debris of hardwood trees (especially birch and maple)—in New York, New England, Ohio, Michigan, North Carolina, Tennessee, and Ontario.

Psilocybe cubensis var. cyanescens (Singer), for- merly *Stropharia cubensis* (Earl): Found from February through November—in compact groups in clearings outside forest areas, on cow or horse dung, in rich pasture soil, on straw, or on sawdust/dung mixture—in Mexico, Cuba, Florida, and other southern states. It grows well on MEA. At 86° F carpophores appear in 4-8 weeks. Thermal death occurs at 104° F.

Carpophores larger than wild specimens can be produced by inoculating a vegetable compost in clay pots with agar grown mycelium, casing with a silica sand/limestone mix, and incubating 4-6 weeks in daylight at 68° F. It does poorly in darkness. It is a potent mushroom and is relatively resistant to contaminants.

Psilocybe cyanescens: Found in autumn—scattered, grouped, or clustered in woods, on earth, among leaves and twigs, and occasionally on decomposing wood—in the northwestern USA.

Psilocybe mexicana: Found from May through October—isolated or sparsely scattered at altitudes from 4500 to 5500 feet (especially in limestone regions) among mosses and herbs, along roadsides, in humid meadows, in cornfields, and near pine forests—in Mexico.

Psilocybe pelliculosa: Found from September through December—scattered, grouped, or clustered on humus and debris in or near conifer forests—in the northwestern USA and as far south as Marin County, California. This is a small but potent species.

Psilocybe quebecensis: Found from summer through late October—scattered in shady areas at forest edges, on sandy soil containing

Psilocybe cyanescens

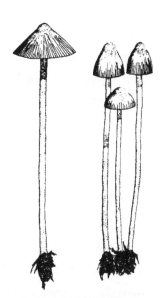

Psilocybe pelliculosa

Psilocybe semilanceata

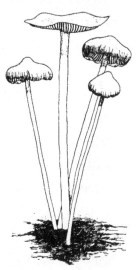

Psilocybe strictipes

Drawing by Michael B. Smith from *Hallucinogenic and Poisonous Mushroom Field Guide* by Gary P. Menser, Ronin Publishing, Inc. Used by permission.

vegetable debris regularly inundated by river flooding, and on decomposing wood and debris (especially birch, alder, fir, and spruce)—in the Quebec area. It thrives at lower temperatures than do other *Psilocybe* species and produces carpophores at air temperatures of 43-59° F.

Psilocybe semilanceata: Found from August through September—often in large groups on soil, among grasses, in clearings, pastures, meadows, forest edges, open conifer woodlands, and on roadsides (but never on dung)—in New York, northern USA, British Columbia, and Europe. Generally regarded as one of the less potent species, it is sometimes quite potent.

Psilocybe strictipes: Found in October—rather clustered on soil or on decomposing wood and debris (of conifers and other trees)—in the northwestern USA (especially in Oregon). It closely resembles *P. baeocystis*, but has a longer stem. It tends to be as visually hallucinogenic as that species and probably contains the same or similar baeocystin alkaloids.

Psilocybe sylvatica: Found in September and October—in small, compact but unclustered groups in woods on leaf mold, on debris (especially beech wood), around stumps and logs (but not usually on them)—from New York to Michigan and as far north as Quebec and Ontario. This mushroom is small and is often mistaken for *P. pelliculosa.*

The species discussed above are only some of the more commonly known ones with hallucinogenic properties. They are recognized among the many psilocybin-bearing mushrooms: 40 species of *Conocybe* (usually found in forests, pastures, gardens, dung areas, sandy soil, ant hills, decayed wood, and charcoal and having a cosmopolitan range); 20 species of *Panaeolus* (found on soil and dung and having a cosmopolitan range); 40 species of *Psilocybe* (found on soil, moss clumps, and organic substrata—such as dung, rotting wood, bagasse, and pear—and ranging from the arctic to the tropics); and 9 species of *Stropharia* (found on soil, dung, and sometimes on leaf mulch and rotting wood and having a fairly cosmopolitan range).

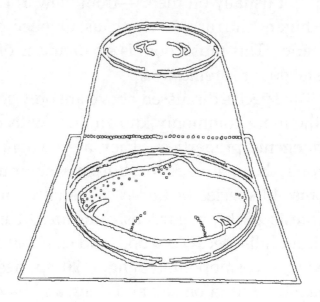

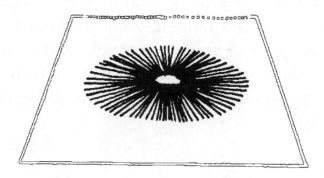

Making a spore print

Drawing by Michael B. Smith from *Hallucinogenic and Poisonous Mushroom Field Guide* by Gary P. Menser, Ronin Publishing, Inc. Used by permission.

Making a Spore Print

A spore print is a collection of spores on a flat surface. It can serve several purposes. It can be used to assist identification of the specimen by observing its color; or if made on a glass slide, by studying the shapes of the spores under a microscope. Mycological identification keys include descriptions of spore prints and microscopic spore features for different species. Spore prints are also the standard method of collecting spores for later germination on agar media. A print from a single mushroom cap contains millions of spores.

The method for making a spore print is as follows. A mushroom with its cap fully opened and its gills exposed is selected. With a sharp sterilized blade the stem is cut off as close to the gills as possible. The cap is placed gills down on a clean, white sheet of paper; on a sheet of glass that just been swabbed with alcohol, or on two or four sterilized microscopic slide glasses. The cap is covered with a clean, inverted bowl or bell jar for 24 hours to prevent drying of the cap and intrusion of foreign organisms. If a good spore print has not formed after this time, the cap is tapped lightly with the flat side of a knife or spatula. This should shake loose many spores. If the print is made on glass, it is covered with another glass sheet immediately after removing the cap in order to prevent contamination. If microscopic slides are used, two slides are placed face to face and the edges are sealed with tape. If paper is used, it is folded several times so that the print is well inside.

Spore prints are also available by mail order. **CAUTION: Extreme care is required about identity of spores.** Spores received from other persons might not be from the species that the sender claims they are. If the sender has misidentified the specimen and the recipient cultivates and ingests mycelia or extractions therefrom, the result may be disastrous.

Pure Culture Technique

The most difficult part of psilocybian mushroom cultivation is the observance of the rules of pure culture technique. These are the sanitary codes of mushroom cultivation. There are usually many varieties of bacteria and fungal spores in our environment; floating in the air, clinging to our hands and clothing, issuing from our mouths with every exhalation. Extreme measures must therefore be taken to keep these out of the mycelial cultures, which could be rapidly overrun. The following points should be diligently observed.

Work should be done in a clean, uncluttered, dust-free room. Immediately before work, the work table is washed and the room is sprayed with disinfectant. Arms, hands, and nails are scrubbed with disinfectant soap. Simple clothing should be worn. A freshly

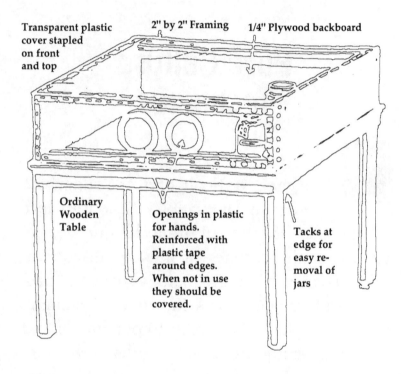

Transparent plastic
cover stapled
on front
and top

2" by 2" Framing

1/4" Plywood backboard

Ordinary
Wooden
Table

Openings in plastic
for hands.
Reinforced with
plastic tape
around edges.
When not in use
they should be
covered.

Tacks at
edge for
easy re-
moval of
jars

Home made inoculation hood

cleaned short-sleeve T-shirt is ideal. Antiseptic mouthwash can be used in addition to covering the mouth and nose with a clean cloth or disposable surgery mask. The hair is covered with a surgical cap or shower cap. No drafts should be present in the room. All windows are closed and all doorjambs stuffed with a towel or rags. No flies, animals, or unneces-

Alchemical Advice

• Before every experiment, you should mentally go through all the processes. Make sure that everything is at hand and that all your equipment is clean.

• Keep an orderly laboratory diary in which all dates, quantities, exact times, and the course of the experiment are exactly noted, including, of course, also all mistakes.

• Let the keynote of your work be the desire to know the wonders of nature and the desire to help others. The highest form of medicine is love, says Paracelsus. If with his experiments the spagyrist [alchemist] does not at the same time devote himself to human spagyrics [alchemy], that is, the perfecting of his personality, everything is but of little value.

• Be aware that you are but an instrument of wise Nature and God.

—from *The Practical Handbook of Plant Alchemy* by Manfred M. Junius sary people should be allowed in the room. Only sterilized equipment should touch the medium or inoculum. One should never lean over the work. All swift movements that may cause a draft should be avoided. If possible a hood should be constructed around the work table or a screen or curtain should surround it. All materials should be kept in order and within reach. All equipment should be kept about three feet away from work. No one should be permitted to enter or exit the room while work is in progress.

The Alchemist in his Lab

Equipment

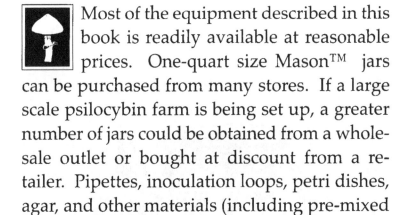Most of the equipment described in this book is readily available at reasonable prices. One-quart size Mason™ jars can be purchased from many stores. If a large scale psilocybin farm is being set up, a greater number of jars could be obtained from a wholesale outlet or bought at discount from a retailer. Pipettes, inoculation loops, petri dishes, agar, and other materials (including pre-mixed media) are found at many scientific supply houses. If petri dishes are not on hand, there are several other containers that can be used.

Baby food jars, 1/4 filled with agar media, are excellent substitutes. Test tubes can be filled 1/3 with hot agar medium, stoppered with cotton, autoclaved, and allowed to cool while standing at a 17° angle. These are known as "slants" and permit a maximum surface area. A wooden rack can easily be constructed to hold the slants at this angle. Baby bottles with

a steam sterilizer can be bought almost any-
where. These come in sets of nine or ten bottles.
The tip of the rubber nipple should be cut off
and a wad of clean cotton pulled through from
the inside leaving about 1/2 inch sticking out.
The bottles are filled 1/3 with agar medium.
After sterilizing, the bottles should be kept at a
17° angle. A large pressure cooker—the type
used for canning and jarring—can be used for
autoclaving Mason™ jars of broth medium.

Preparation of Media

There are two types of media that must be prepared. A jello-like *agar* medium (PDYA or MEA) is used for the initial inoculation. After the mycelium has developed in this medium, it is transferred to a *liquid broth* medium (PDY) to allow for maximum growth.

PDYA (Potato Dextrose Yeast Agar): 250 grams of unpeeled potatoes are washed and sliced 1/8 inch thick. The slices are washed several more times in cool tap water until the water is clear, drained in a colander, and rinsed once with distilled water. Then the potato slices are cooked in distilled water until tender. The cooking liquids are strained through a flannel cloth or several layers of cheesecloth and are collected in a flask. The potatoes are rinsed several more times with distilled water. These rinse waters are added to the liquid in the flask, and the potatoes are discarded. Enough distilled water is added to the flask to make one liter. The liquid is brought to a boil and 15 grams of agar, 10 grams of dextrose, and 1.5 grams of yeast extract are added. The agar must be added slowly and carefully to prevent boiling over. While the liquid is hot, it is poured into sterilized petri dishes or any other sterilized containers. Each should be filled about halfway.

MEA (Malt Extract Agar): To one liter of gently boiling distilled water are added 20 grams of malt extract, 20 grams of agar (slowly and carefully to prevent boiling over), 100 mg of potassium phosphate dibasic (K_2HPO_4), and 100 mg of calcium carbonate. While still hot, the liquid is poured into sterilized culture dishes.

PDY broth: This broth is made in exactly the same manner as PDYA except the agar is omitted. Sterilized Mason™ jars are filled half way with the hot or cool liquid.

Sterilization

All utensils used in the cultivation of the mycelia must be sterilized by heat before use. Glassware must be boiled in water for 30 minutes. Metalware used repeatedly must be held in a flame until glowing and then allowed a moment to cool before making contact with any cultures or specimens. When the inoculation loop has been used to transfer a fragment of mycelium, it must be flame sterilized after the medium has been poured.

The following sterilization process is known as "autoclaving." Containers no more than half full with medium are placed in a canning-type pressure cooker. The lids of these must be loose enough to allow escapage of internal pressure. Otherwise the containers may crack. The lid of the pressure cooker is sealed and the stopcock valve is left open. The cooker is brought to boiling using high heat until thick steam comes through the vent. The stopcock is closed and the pressure is allowed rise to 15-20 lbs. (250° F) for 30 minutes. This will destroy any foreign spores or life-forms. A higher temperature or longer period, however, could cause the dextrose or maltose sugars to caramelize. This would inhibit the growth and psilocybin production of the mycelium.

When the autoclave period is finished, the heat is turned off and the cooker is allowed to cool to room temperature. The stopcock is not released until everything has thoroughly cooled, or else the sudden change in pressure will cause the containers to boil over. Any containers that have cracked during sterilization are discarded. All containers of medium are kept at room temperature for three days to see if any foreign molds develop. If this occurs, the contaminated medium is discarded, and the jars are thoroughly cleaned and sterilized before being used again.

Starting the Culture

Upon obtaining one or more specimens of a psilocybin bearing mushroom, one can begin to cultivate as much of the hallucinogen as desired. Any part of the fungus can be used for inoculation. If the spores are used, consideration must be given to the natural life cycle of the mushroom. A single cap contains millions of spores, and any one of these will germinate in the medium to form a mycelium. But this mycelium will consist of what is known as monokaryotic tissue. Such a mycelial organism will grow for a while, but unless it mates with another compatible monokaryotic mycelium and forms a dikaryotic structure, it will eventually perish.

The process for developing a culture from spores is as follows. The spores are scraped from the print into about 10 ml of sterilized water, and the solution is vigorously shaken. Another 90 ml of sterilized water is added, and the solution is shaken again. There will be millions of spores in this solution. Several petri dishes—or other suitable containers as previously described—containing sterilized agar medium should be ready for inoculation. The lid on each container is lifted slightly, and with a sterilized pipette or syringe, a drop of this spore water is placed on three or four different parts of the agar surface. The container is covered immediately, and the dish is left to stand at room temperature for 3-5 days.

Radial growths of monokaryotic mycelium will occur at each inoculation point. When any two mycelia have grown to the point of making contact with each other, mating (somatogamy) will take place. Within a few days these united mycelia will have become dikaryotic organisms. Any portion of this mycelial tissue can now be used to seed new cultures as described later.

If a portion of one of the carpophores gathered in the field is used to inoculate the agar, mating is not necessary. The tissue of the mature fungus is already dikaryotic. To avoid contamination only inner tissues are used. The mushroom cap is placed gills-down on a clean work table at least three feet away from any equipment. All dirt and slime is wiped from the cap with a cotton swab, and its whole surface is cleaned with a 7% iodine solution. The cap is pinned to the table top by inserting three dissecting needles at equilateral points. An X-acto blade is sterilized by flame and allowed to cool for a moment. The outer skin is then carved from the mushroom. Tiny pieces of the inner mushroom flesh—about the size of a match head—are cut out. Each piece is skewered with the blade point. The lid of a petri dish is raised slightly. The tissue is pressed firmly into the agar surface, and the lid is closed immediately. All inoculated dishes are placed on the incubation shelf at room temperature. The mycelium must breath as it grows, so the lids must not be capped too tightly.

When the radial growths of mycelia appear on the agar surface (3-5 days) these stock cultures are ready for transferring to the broth jars. If any stock cultures are not going to be used immediately, they are placed with tightened lids under refrigeration. They can be kept this way for about a year.

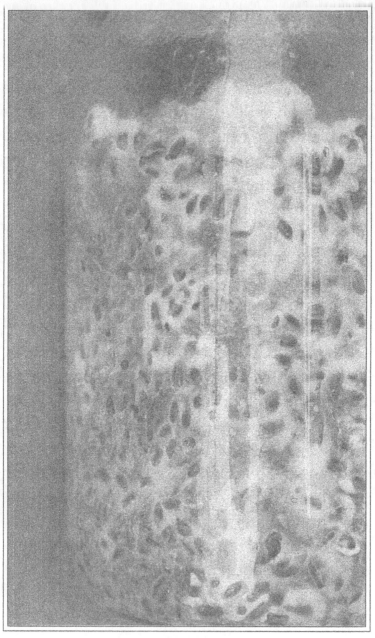

Adam Gottlieb

Mycelium cultivation jar

Raising Crop Cultures of Mycelia

 The next step is selecting the most vigorous mycelia in the dishes. This means the largest and fastest growing specimens not contaminated by foreign molds. Contaminants are not difficult to detect, because their appearance differs greatly from that of mycelia. Mycelia are pure white fibrous mats sometimes having a light bluish tinge. Contaminants may appear as rapid-growing, tiny, white circular spots with bluish-green centers; surface scums; or fuzzy clusters of either gray, black, yellow, green, or blue color. If any contaminants appear in any of the culture dishes, those cultures are discarded.

When the dishes containing the choicest mycelia have been selected, the mycelia are transferred from the agar-based stock cultures to the liquid PDY broth cultivation jars. These jars should have been prepared and sterilized three days before transferring and allowed to stand at room temperature during this time in order to test the effectiveness of the sterilization. All broths which contain growths are discarded. The uncontaminated jars are now ready for inoculation.

The room is sprayed and the work area is cleaned as described under pure culture techniques. The outside parts of the stock dishes and culture jars are also sprayed. The lid of a stock dish is lifted just enough, and a fragment of mycelium is picked up with an inoculation loop that has been flame-sterilized and allowed a moment to cool. The cover of a jar is lifted. The mycelium fragment is placed in the broth, and the jar is covered immediately. This is repeated until all jars have been inoculated. All unused stock cultures are refrigerated.

The jars are covered tightly and shaken well to disperse the inoculum throughout the broth. This also aerates the medium; the mycelium needs oxygen for life support and growth. The lids are loosened again, and the jars are placed on the growing shelf for 10-12 days at 70-75° F. If species other than *Psilocybe cubensis* are used, the temperature is adjusted accordingly. Every 2-3 days the covers are tightened, and the jars are shaken to aerate and disperse the mycelium. Afterwards, the covers are loosened again, and the jars are returned to the shelf.

The process of growth can be followed with a saccharimeter. The maximum growth and highest percentage of psilocybin occurs about four days after all of the broth's sugar content has been used up. The mycelium should be harvested at this time. Any jars that cannot be harvested on that day should be refrigerated until this can be done.

Harvesting the Alchemical Fruit

Harvesting and Drying

The medium of each jar is filtered through a clean flannel cloth. The mycelial material is collected from the cloth and placed in a Pyrex™ baking dish. The same is done with each jar of mycelium until each baking dish is about 1/3 full with mycelia. The collected mycelium is then dried in an oven at a temperature no higher than 200° F. An oven thermometer should be used, because the temperature indications on the oven knob may not be accurate. The mycelium should be checked periodically. When the material first appears to have dried, the heat is turned off and the mycelium is left in the oven until it has cooled. This ensures the evaporation of residual moisture. Each cultivation jar should yield 50-100 grams of wet mycelium. Fresh mycelium contains about 90% water, so this amount should dry down to 5-10 grams of crumbly material.

The Spirit of the Mushrooms

On the evening of 11 October 1962, near the remote Mexican village of Huautla de Jiménez . . . the Swiss chemist Albert Hofmann gave 30 milligrams of synthetic psilocybine each to María Sabina, her daughter, and another Mazatec shaman. Hofmann also gave 10 milligrams of psilocybine to R. Gordon Wasson, who seven years earlier had become the first outsider ever purposely to ingest the sacred mushrooms of Mexico, when he was initiated into the sacred Mystery by María Sabina. Hofmann had obtained specimens of María Sabina's mushrooms through Wasson, and in his laboratory at Sandoz Ltd. in Basel had succeeded in isolating and characterizing the active principles, which he named psilocybin(e) and psilocin(e). Hofmann had prepared both drugs synthetically in Switzerland, and came to Mexico with "the spirit of the mushrooms in the form of pills," in hopes of giving the novel drug to a shaman experienced in the use of the mushrooms.

—from *Pharmacotheon* by Jonathan Ott

Extraction

The dried mycelial material is crumbled and pulverized, and each 100 mg of this is combined in a flask with 10 ml of absolute methanol. The flask is placed in a hot water bath for four hours. The liquids are filtered with suction through filter paper in a Buchner funnel with Celite™ to prevent clogging. The filtrate liquids are collected and saved. The slurry (the mush in the filter paper) is heated two more times in methanol as before. The liquids of the three extractions are filtered and joined together.

To be certain that all of the alkaloids have been extracted, a small extraction of a portion of the used slurry is tested with Keller's Reagent (glacial acetic acid, ferrous chloride, and concentrated sulfuric acid). If there is a violet indication, alkaloids are still present and further extraction is in order.

In an open beaker the liquids are evaporated to total dryness with a hot water bath or by applying a hair dryer. All traces of methanol must be removed. The remaining residue should contain a 25-50% psilocybin/psilocin mixture.

Greater purification can be achieved, but it would require other solvents and chromatography equipment and is hardly necessary. Each 100 grams of dried mycelium should yield about 2 grams of extracted material. This should contain at least 500 mg of a psilocybin/psilocin mixture or about fifty 10 mg doses.

Theoretically, psilocin should have the same effect upon the user as psilocybin. The only difference between the two is that the latter has a phosphate bond which disappears immediately after assimilation in the body. In other words, in the body psilocybin turns into psilocin.

Psilocybin is a fairly stable compound, but psilocin is very susceptible to oxidation. It is best to keep the extracted material in a dry air tight container under refrigeration. A sack of silica-gel can be placed in the container to capture any moisture that may enter.

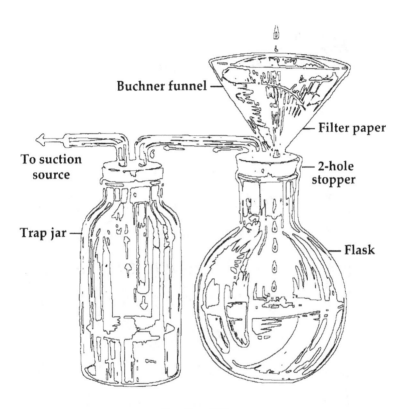

Buchner funnel

Filter paper

To suction
source

2-hole
stopper

Trap jar

Flask

Suction filter

"Come! my head's free
at last!" said Alice in a
tone of delight, which
changed into alarm in
another moment, when she
found that her shoulders
were nowhere to be seen:
she looked down upon an
immense length of neck,
which seemed to rise like
a stalk out of a sea
of green leaves that
lay far below her.

—from *Alice's Adventures Under Ground*
by Lewis Carroll

Dosage

The standard dose of psilocybin or psilocin for a 150 lb. person is 6-20 mg. The average dose is 10 mg. The crude alkaloid extraction process just described yields a brownish crystalline powder that is about 25% pure. Each Mason™ jar usually contains about 50 grams of wet mycelium. After drying, this would result in about 5 grams of material. The crude material extracted from this would contain 25-35 mg. of psilocybin/psilocin or roughly 2-3 doses.

This yield may vary to some extent depending upon several factors. Many species contain less of these alkaloids than does *Psilocybe cubensis*, and the alkaloidal content of this species may vary in different strains. Cultivation conditions have a lot to do with yield too. Higher temperatures (75° F) cause more rapid growth but lesser psilocybin content than do lower temperatures (70° F). Each new batch of extracted material must be tested to determine the proper distribution of dosages. Depending upon the potency of the mycelia and how well the extraction was conducted, the dose may range between 25 and 100 mg. The dose also varies for different individuals.

Large Scale Production

 The techniques and procedures described in this book could be employed to cultivate modest supplies of psilocybin for personal use, or they could be expanded for the large scale production of many thousands of doses per week. The diagram on the following page shows one way in which a small 10 x 15 foot room with standard 8 foot ceilings could be set up to produce a continuing yield of about 5000 doses per week.

The stock culture shelves here are 1 foot deep and 5 feet long. Each holds twenty 15 cm petri dishes. If the shelving is spaced six inches apart, there can be as many as 16 shelves stacked in this space. This would allow for up to 300 stock culture dishes going at one time. The crop culture shelves are stacked ten inches apart, accommodating one quart size Mason™ jars and giving ten shelves. With the dimensions of the room depicted in this diagram,

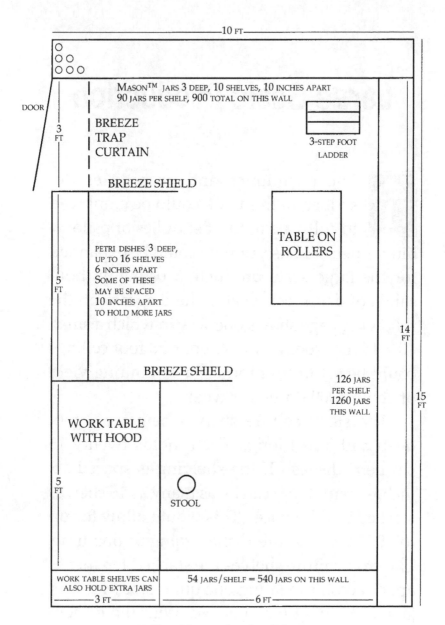

Psilocybin production laboratory

this much shelving could hold about 2700 jars (3 deep and 3 per running foot).

The entire room—walls, ceiling and shelving—are painted with a white, glossy kitchen enamel. This is not only an important sanitary measure, but also improves the efficiency and even distribution of light in the room.

Lighting is provided by a few banks of wide spectrum fluorescent tubes fairly evenly distributed across the ceiling and turned on for 10-12 hours regularly each day. These are great dust catchers, however, and must be wiped clean periodically.

The work table is also be painted with a hard, smooth, white finish. If the table is of metal, a small, clean cutting board must be provided on which to pin down mushroom caps when dissecting them. Shelf boards on the wall left of the table may extend above the table to provide space for storage of work equipment and ready containers. A hood is constructed around the table to protect this space from dust.

A fume hood with a flu vent and spark-free exhaust fan is constructed over the extraction table to remove toxic and combustible methanol vapors. Extraction is preferably conducted in another room. If the cultivation room is used for extraction while cultures are growing, care must be taken that the heat from the extraction processes does not alter the room temperature. The fume hood would help by carrying off much of the heat.

A vinyl shower curtain is hung to the right of the table to shield the work area from breezes when anyone enters or exits the room. Another vinyl curtain is hung just inside the entrance to serve as a dust trap. A person entering would close the door behind him before pulling the curtain aside—and vice versa on exiting.

The floor is white vinyl or asphalt tile or could be painted white and coated with varathane or polyurethane. There is no cloth or carpeting in the room except for a supply of clean work clothing and surgical masks.

The only other items in the room are a stool at the work table, a three-step ladder for reaching the upper shelves, and a small table on rollers on which to place jars and dishes when making the rounds of the shelves.

Production Schedule

Unless one has a large staff of assistants, it would be impossible to innoculate 2,700 jars in one work session. After getting used to the work, one could do about 100 jars an hour. The procedure used would be to set up a continuous rotation of inoculations. Working about 3 hours a day, about 225 jars could be inoculated each session. All 2700 jars could be inoculated in 12 days. Sections of shelving would be divided into groups of 225 jars, and these sections would be labeled with the date and approximate time of inoculation. The work schedule for cultivation would be as follows:

Day	Inoculate	Shake	Harvest	Reinoculate
Mon.	Group A			
Tues.	B			
Wed.	C	Group A		
Thurs.	D	B		
Fri.	E	A & C		
Sat.	F	B & D		
Sun.	G	A, C & E		
Mon.	H	B, D & F		
Tues.	I	A, C, E & G		
Wed.	J	B, D, F & H		
Thurs.	K	A, C, E, G & I		
Fri.	L	B, D, F, H & J		
Sat.	Commence Reinoculation	C, E, G, I & K	Group A	Group A2
Sun.		D, F, H, J & L	B	B2
Mon.		E, G, I, K & A2	C	C2
Tues.		F, H, J, L & B2	D	D2
Etc.		Etc.	Etc.	Etc.

This represents the first two weeks of the continuous cultivation cycle. The continuation of this schedule is obvious: shaking every other day; harvesting approximately every 12 days; and resterilizing, refilling with fresh medium, autoclaving, and reinoculating the jars liberated by the day's harvest. If the total number of jars is 2700, each group would consist of about 225 jars. This same schedule could, of course, be adapted to any total number of jars.

Drying of mycelia is done within a few hours after harvesting. Otherwise, enzymes in the material will begin to destroy the active alkaloids. Once dried, the material can be

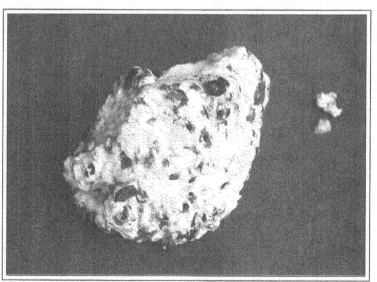

Harvested and dried mycelial material

stored in a cool, dark, dry place until enough daily harvests have been accumulated to do an extraction. If the mycelia cannot be dried right away, it can be kept in a refrigerator for a day or two or in a freezer for longer times.

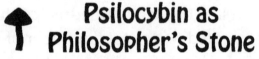

Psilocybin as Philosopher's Stone

What is needed is a new drug which will relieve and console our suffering species without doing more harm in the long run than it does good in the short. Such a drug must be potent in minute doses and synthesizable. . . . It must be less toxic than opium or cocaine, less likely to produce undesirable social consequences than alcohol or the barbiturates, less inimical to heart and lungs than the tars and nicotine of cigarettes. And, on the positive side, it should produce changes in consciousness more interesting, more intrinsically valuable than mere sedation or dreaminess, delusions of omnipotence or release from inhibition.

—from *The Doors of Perception*
by Aldous Huxley

Maintaining a Psilocybin Farm

Fresh inoculum can come from stock culture dishes kept under refrigeration. If these should become depleted, healthy strains of mycelium from the crop cultures can be used to inoculate sterilized agar media in the dishes. The crop culture jar is shaken violently to break up the mycelium. Then drops of the liquid are transferred to autoclaved petri dishes of unused agar medium with a sterilized pipette and left to grow as before. If this reinoculation of stock cultures from existing crops is continued over a long period of time, the strain will eventually weaken due to what is called the senescence factor. To avoid this, the media used in the stock dishes are alternated. If PDA is used the first time, MEA is used the second time, and PDA is used again the third time, and so on.

Bob Harris

Mushroom primordia

Fruiting the Mushroom

People who cultivate psilocybian mushrooms initiate fruiting of the mushroom after the mycelium has developed rather than immediately extract the psilocybin. Great pleasure is derived from nurturing a mushroom from inception to fruition.

There are several methods for initiating carpophores, or fruitin bodies. To bring forth the fruit of the mushroom, success will be more easily achieved if a spawning medium other than a liquid broth is used to cultivate the mycelium. Some people recreate natural growing conditions through the use of compost, whereas apartment cultivators often prefer the ease and low cost of a grain medium. Rye is the most commonly used grain medium because of its low cost and availability, and because its kernels don't clump together like other grains do. The grain medium is sterilized and inoculated using the same methods described earlier for inoculating the liquid broth cultivation jars.

Once the mycelium has completely colonized the grain medium, it is ready for casing. Casing is a layer of organic matter which covers the substrate (in this case, the colonized grain medium). The function of the casing is to prevent the surface of the mycelium from drying out. The casing material must be porous enough to allow for sufficient aeration, yet it must also be able to retain moisture. Some mycologists recommend the use of a peat moss casing with the addition of chalk or limestone flour in order to balance the highly acidic pH of the peat moss. Home-growers simply use sterilized soil or vermiculite.

Before the substrate is cased, a suitable growing container must be chosen. The easiest method is to leave the colonized grain medium in the cultivation jars and simply case the surface. The fruiting mushroom bodies will then grow out of the mouth of the jar. (Use of a wide mouth jar makes it easier to remove the mushrooms when the time comes). There are a few disadvantages with this method: mushrooms frequently and unsuccessfully attempt to grow between the grain and the glass surface of the jar; the low ratio of surface area

to grain depth means that much of the mycelium is unable to form carpophores; and it is
more difficult to water and pick mushrooms
without damaging developing pinheads, or pri-
mordial mushrooms. Alternative containers include plastic trays, trash bags, baking dishes,
plastic lined cardboard boxes, or aquarium
tanks. If one opts for one of these alternative
containers, the colonized grain medium is simply transferred to the new containers and covered with a casing layer.

A growing environment must be created in
order to initiate fruiting of the mushroom.
There are five factors which are involved in
creating the optimum fruiting environment:
humidity, temperature, fresh air, CO2 levels,
and light. And there are three stages of carpophore development, each of which has its own
special environmental requirements. Therefore,
a growing chamber must be constructed that
can meet the demands of each of the following
stages:

Casing Colonization

During this stage the casing material is colonized by the mycelium. The humidity of the

growing chamber is kept very high (around
90%). A humidifier can be used for this purpose. If this is not possible, it is essential to
maintain the moisture content of the substrate
and casing through light but regular watering.
The optimal growing temperatures are different for each psilocybian species (*Psilocybe
cubensis* does best at 84-86° F). At this stage
there should be no light and no fresh air. The
casing layer should be made to resemble
"mountains and valleys" in order to increase
its surface area and aid in the dispersion of
carbon dioxide.

Pinhead Initiation

This stage starts the actual fruiting process
with the initiation of pinheads. When the mycelium has uniformly broken through the surface of the casing's "valleys," it is time for initiation. Pinhead initiation is achieved through
a drop in temperature, a reduction of carbon
dioxide (through the introduction of fresh air),
and the presence of light (via natural daylight
or an artificial 12 hour on/off cycle). The humidity is maintained at its previous   level.
When using artificial lighting, a grow-lux type

artificial light high in blue spectra is most ef-
fective. It is important to carefully maintain
the growing environment at this time. Abrupt
changes in humidity or temperature will dis-
rupt the growth of the mushrooms. Too much
fresh air can reduce the humidity and alter the
temperature of the growing environment. The
casing can be misted with water. However, if
it is too forceful, developing pinheads may be
damaged or destroyed.

Primordia Development

Once the pinheads have grown to the size
of a pea, the humidity is dropped to 85-90%.
Small primordia will begin to develop. These
baby mushrooms look like small penises and
will continue to grow over a period of a week.
The mushrooms are harvested just after the
partial veil ruptures. The psilocybin content of
the mushrooms is highest at this stage in the
carpophore's growth. If spores are required,
one can let the carpophore continue to grow
until the cap becomes slightly upturned or until there is a slight purplish color around the
base of the mushroom indicating that sporing
has already begun.

Constructing a Growing Chamber

A growing chamber can be contructed from a plastic lined box, an aquarium, or a styrofoam cooler. The main requirements are that it be insulated and well sealed in order to prevent loss of temperature and humidity. Humidity is provided by a humidifier or by regular misting. The required temperature is provided through steam, a heating pad underneath the chamber, or an overhead light. Use of a heating pad or light will tend to lower humidity, so caution is used to maintain proper humidity. Fresh air can be introduced via the humidifier or when the chamber is opened for misting. CO_2 is removed through holes at the bottom of the chamber (CO_2 is heavier than air and will sink to the bottom of the chamber) or by opening the chamber and fanning the interior.

How to Use the Magic

When mushrooms were scarce and obtainable only with difficulty, the main question was how to get them. Once got, they were used on special occasions with care. Now that we have the mushrooms and have them in plenty, the question is how to use them. Psychoactive mushrooms are special gifts of nature, magical fruits of the earth with power to help us understand ourselves and change us. But that magic is volatile. It can evaporate in an instant if . . . we use mushrooms frivolously or thoughtlessly. . . .

—from **"Reflections on Psychedelic Mycophagy" by Andrew Weil**

Legal Update

by Richard Glen Boire, Attorney

Dr. Alexander Shulgin, the famous psychopharmacologist who re-created MDMA and brought forth over 200 other mind-manifesting substances, has said that psychedelics are dolphins caught in the tuna net of anti-drug laws. His point is perhaps nowhere better exemplified than with psilocybin and psilocin, the active chemicals in the sacred mushrooms known as *teonanácatl* in the Aztec language. For over two millennia, entheogenic mushrooms have played the central role in a religion whose participants consume these mushrooms to experience the divine. These mushrooms are a true sacrament, not a symbolic one. Individuals and underground religious groups worldwide continue this practice today, despite an all-out government assault on their religion.

The book you are now reading is dangerous. Dangerous to the interests of those authorities who would like nothing better than to replace true religion with a placebo. This book is also dangerous because it describes a process that, if followed in the United States, could land one in a federal penitentiary.

In his chapter titled "Psilocybin and the Law," Gottlieb does a good job of outlining the broader contours of the laws facing people who contemplate growing entheogenic mushrooms. To put it simply, just about any action involving the substances psilocybin or psilocin, is a crime under federal and state laws. Both substances have been placed in Schedule I of the federal Controlled Substance Act, and all 50 states have followed suit by outlawing the possession, manufacture, distribution, transportation, importation and exportation of these substances.

Under federal law, and under all state laws that I'm aware of, no mushrooms in the genus *Psilocybe* are outlawed by name. Gottlieb is incorrect when he states that *P. mexicana* is explicitly outlawed—an inaccuracy I've often seen repeated in the literature. Although no *Psilocybe* mushrooms are explicitly outlawed, don't jump to the conclusion that it's safe to possess or grow them; such is not the case.

Thousands of people have been arrested for "crimes" involving entheogenic mushrooms.

How are the authorities able to arrest people when there's no law that explicitly outlaws these mushrooms? By legal hocus-pocus and pettifoggery, that's how.

The authorities point to federal and state law provisions that were designed to punish drug dealers and manufacturers who attempt to increase their profits by diluting drugs (e.g., cocaine or methamphetamine) with various cutting agents, or who add binding agents to their drug (e.g., MDMA) in order to sell it in tablet form. The federal law provision on this subject outlaws "any material, compound, mixture, or preparation, which contains any quantity of" a controlled substance.

Under this provision, ten grams of an innocuous legal substance like vitamin B12, is treated exactly like ten grams of a controlled substance if the vitamin B12 has any amount of an illegal substance mixed into it. It is clear that Congress designed this provision to increase the punishment of drug dealers and manufacturers who increase their sales and profits by stretching drugs or dealing in tablets. Nevertheless, in order to argue that entheogenic mushrooms are illegal, federal and state prosecutors have interpreted this provision in a preposterous manner. Relying on this provision, prosecutors make the bizarre and ultra-reductionistic argument that entheogenic mushrooms are illegal "containers" or "mixtures" of the controlled substances psilocybin and psilocin.

This absurd argument denies the undeniable: that living organisms are very different than inert cutting and binding agents. This theory outlaws any life-form that naturally produces a controlled substance, thereby elevating federal law over Nature herself. Under such a theory, not only would many common plants be outlawed (morning glories for instance), but our own brains would also be outlawed because they naturally produce and contain the controlled substance N,N-dimethyltryptamine (DMT)!

Whether or not entheogenic mushrooms are properly considered illegal mixtures or containers of controlled substances, it is clear that *extracting* psilocybin or psilocin from mushrooms is unlawful. Federal and state laws consider it "manufacturing" a controlled substance to extract it from a substance of natural origin, such as a mushroom or its mycelium. Consequently, following the extraction process detailed in this book is illegal in the United States. Additionally, California is unique in explicitly outlawing the cultivation—with or without eventual extraction—of any "spores or mycelium capable of producing mushrooms . . . which contain" psilocybin or psilocin.

This leads to a quick note on the legality of spore prints from entheogenic mushrooms. The "mixture/container" argument is clearly not applicable to the spores of these mushrooms. The spores do not contain psilocybin or psilocin. These substances are first produced, in most cases, when the mushroom enters its mycelial growth stage. Therefore, spore prints of entheogenic mushrooms are legal under federal law and in every state but one. As stated above, California is unique in passing laws which expressly address the legality of some mushroom spore prints. Under California laws, it is a crime to transport, import into California, sell, furnish, or give away, mushroom spores for the purpose of using them to cultivate mushrooms that naturally produce psilocybin or psilocin.

This has been a brief summary of the current state of the law with respect to entheogenic mushrooms and their chemical constituents. Let us hope that in the not too distant future, these psychedelic dolphins will be cut free from the anti-drug nets and we shall swim freely among them. Nature is, after all, our host.

Richard Glen Boire, Esq.

Richard Glen Boire is a criminal defense attorney practicing in Northern California. He is the publisher of *The Entheogen Law Reporter* and the author of *Sacred Mushrooms and the Law* and *Marijuana Law*.

Recommended Reading

Growing Wild Mushrooms, Bob Harris, Homestead Book Company, 1992. This classic is a clear well illustrated guide to several methods of cultivating psychoactive mushrooms by the inventor of the Homestead Mushroom Kit.

Hallucinogenic and Poisonous Mushroom Field Guide, Gary P. Menser, Ronin Publishing, 1996. This is a clear and precise guide to the hallucinogenic mushrooms that grow in the United States and the poisonous species with which they are most easily confused. A reliable reference for beginners.

The Mushroom Cultivator: A Practical Guide to Growing Mushrooms at Home, Paul Stamets and J.S. Chilton, Agarikon Press, 1983. This comprehensive tome contains in great detail everything that a person needs to know about the successful cultivation of mushrooms. The informative text is copiously illustrated with lots of black & white and color photographs. This book is for the serious mycologist.

Psilocybin Mushrooms of the World, Paul Stamets, Ten Speed Press, 1996. Lavishly illustrated with color photographs, this guide fully describes nearly 100 species, including close relatives, poisonous look-alikes, and many new species not seen in previous works.

Suppliers

Homestead Book Company
P.O. Box 31608
Seattle, WA 98103
Phone: (800) 426-6777, (206) 782-4532
E-mail: DaveT@HomesteadBK.com

Homestead Book Company sells a *P. cubensis* Mushroom Kit and *P. cubensis* spore prints as well as books and videos about mushroom cultivation.

Mushroom People
560 Farm Rd.
P.O. Box 220
Summertown, TN 38483-0220
Phone: (800) 386-4496, (615) 964-2200
Fax: (800) 692-6329
E-mail: mushroom@gaia.org
Website: www.gaia.org/farm/mushroom

They sell a wide variety of cultivation supplies and a large selection of books on the cultivation, field identification, and medicinal properties of mushrooms. They *do not* sell any psychoactive spores or cultures. Call for a free catalog.

The ShroomKing
P.O. Box 17444
Seattle, WA 98107

Shroom King sells *P. cubensis* spore syringes.

Fungi Perfecti

P.O. Box 7634
Olympia, WA 98507
Phone: (800) 780-9126, (360) 426-9292
Fax: (360) 426-9377
Email: mycomedia@aol.com
Website: www.fungi.com

Fungi Perfecti is a family owned business dedicated to promoting the cultivation of high quality gourmet and medicinal mushrooms. They sell a wide variety of laboratory and growing room equipment and supplies. They *do not* sell any psychoactive spores or cultures. They request that individuals do not call them with questions concerning psychoactive mushrooms.

Hemp B.C.

504-21 Water St.
Vancouver, B.C.
Canada V6B 1A1
Phone: (800) 330-HEMP, (604) 669-9052
Fax: (604) 669-9038
Website: www.hempbc.com

Hemp BC sells *Psilocybe cubensis* spore syringe, mycelium jar, mycelium on agar, spore print, and the complete Homestead Mushroom Kit.

Legendary Ethnobotanical Resources (LER)

P.O. Box 1676
Coconut Grove, FL 33233
Phone: (305) 649-9997
Website: www.shadow.net/~heruka

LER sells *P. cubensis* spore prints. Send $3.00 for a catalog.

Mycotech
P.O. Box 4647
Seattle, WA 98104
Phone: (206) 364-4851

Mycotech sells a mushroom kit, compost, cultivation supplies, and *P. cubensis* spores. Write or call for a free catalog.

Pacific Exotic Spora
P.O. Box 11611
Honolulu, HI 96828

Pacific Exotic Spora sells an unusual variety of spores: Hawaiian *Copelandia cyanescens*, Hawaiian *Panaeolus cyanescens*, *Psilocybe cubensis* (Amazonian), *Psilocybe cubensis* (Tasmanian), and *Psilocybe tampanensis*. Send $2.00 for a catalog.

Psylocybe Fanaticus
P.O. Box 22009
Seattle, WA 98122
Website: www.Fanaticus.com

PF has created a technique for growing magic mushrooms using common kitchen utensils and easy to get supplies (small jars, powdered rice, vermiculite, and an aquarium). They sell *P. cubensis* spore syringes and instructions for the PF TEK method of growing mushrooms. Send $2.00 and a SASE for a catalog.

Syzygy
P.O. Box 619
Honaunau, HI 96726

Syzygy sells *P. cubensis* spore prints.

TELR
Richard Glen Boire's Quarterly Legal Update on Shamanic Inebriants

Since time immemorial humans have used entheogenic substances as powerful tools for achieving spiritual insight and understanding. In the twentieth century, however, many of these most powerful of religious and epistemological tools were declared illegal in the United States and their users decreed criminals. The shaman has been outlawed. It is the purpose of *The Entheogen Law Reporter (TELR)* to provide the latest information and commentary on the interspace of entheogenic substances and the law.

TELR is a micro-circulation publication funded solely by subscription. Presently, no outside advertising is accepted. A one-year (4-issue) subscription for individuals remains $25 within the USA, and $35 internationally. Institutional subscriptions are $55 worldwide.

Subscriber information is strictly confidential and will be released only under court order. Your name will not be sold or given away.

Subscribe Me !

Name: _____   State: _____

Street: _____   Zip Code: _____

City: _____   E-Mail: _____

Mail cash, check or money order to:
spectral mindustries
POB 73401-PP, DAVIS/CA 95617-3401

TELR

LAW ¡ POLICY ¡ COMMENTARY

AND

CONTROL THEORY

CONCERNING

SHAMANIC INEBRIANTS

Sacred Mushrooms and the Law

This is the only book covering the legal landscape underlying psychedelic mushrooms and their active principles.

Written by Richard Glen Boire, this completely expanded and updated second edition provides practical tactical information never before accessible to the layperson.

All federal and state laws concerning psilocybin, psilocin, and psilocybian mushrooms are covered. Easy-to-use charts clearly spell out the potential punishments for those so daring as to defy governmental edicts.

Richard Glen Boire's manual on the current legal status of psilocybin/psilocin provides valuable information to anyone caught in the Kafkaesque *danse macabre* of "preparing their defense."
-- Terence McKenna --

Sacred Mushrooms & The Law
$12.95

www.ingramcontent.com/pod-product-compliance
Lightning Source LLC
Jackson TN
JSHW080205141224
75386JS00029B/1061